THE FIRST AMERICAN SLAVES
THE HISTORY AND ABOLITION OF SLAVERY

Civil Rights Books for Children
Children's History Books

BABY PROFESSOR
EDUCATION KIDS

Speedy Publishing LLC

40 E. Main St. #1156

Newark, DE 19711

www.speedypublishing.com

Copyright 2017

Slavery will always be a part of American history. Fortunately, your generation will only have to learn about it by reading about it. From their arrival in 1619 to the writing of the Emancipation Proclamation by President Lincoln in 1863 freeing the slaves, there is so much to learn. You will read about some of the events leading up to their freedom in this book.

WHEN DID SLAVERY BEGIN IN THE AMERICAS?

In 1619, the first slaves of the American settlements arrived in Jamestown Virginia via a Dutch boat. Approximately 600,000 more arrived, mostly to perform work in cotton and tobacco fields.

According the Constitution, they were considered three-fifths a person under a state's population count which determines the number of Congressmen representing it. Some of them were treated well, but others horribly. Sometimes they would be beat, branded, whipped, imprisoned, and burned.

Their children would become property of the owner, sometimes sold to different owners without permission or knowledge of the parents. Some of the black people that were free and lived in the South owned slaves.

WHERE DID THEY COME FROM?

....

They were transported from Africa on ships under atrocious conditions. Mostly coming from the ports on the west coast of Africa where the slave trade currently existed. Due to starvation and diseases several of them would die during this trip. They would be packed and chained, not being able to move.

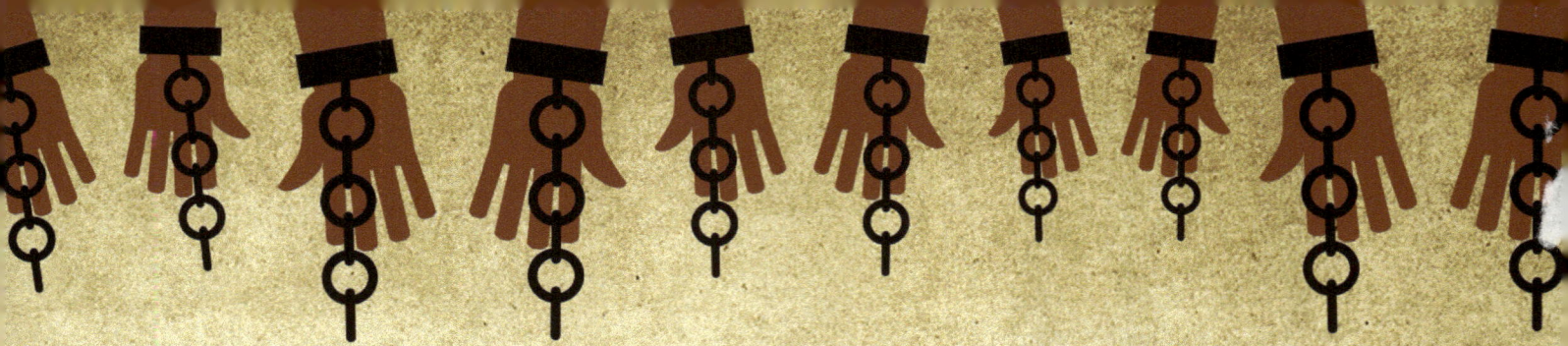

CODES

....

Laws were establishing within the colonies about them designated as slave codes. These codes included laws regarding punishment to the slaves trying to escape.

Under these codes, it was illegal to teach them to read, assist in hiding, and it was illegal to give them money in exchange for work. They could not have weapons, they could not relocate from their owner's plantation, and they could not act as to harm a white person.

UNDERGROUND RAILROAD

....

They were able to escape North via the Underground Railroad. This was a group of people, homes, and hideouts helping them to escape to the North without anyone knowing.

U sing the Underground Railroad, approximately 100,000 slaves escaped between 1810 and 1856. The Underground Railroad was not a real railroad. It was given this name and was considered a way for people to escape.

The people leading them through the routes were known as conductors. There were places along the way for them to hide known as depots or stations. Stockholders were people that helped them by providing food and money. Working as conductors, people would provide safety for the them along the railroad.

Harriet Tubman, after escaping via the railroad, was one of many that escaped and came back to help more escape. Quakers and other white persons who thought slavery was not right also helped others to escape.

Travel with the Underground Railroad was not easy and could be dangerous. They sometimes would travel at night by foot. The people trying to help them escape could also be in danger. Conductors would be killed by hanging if they were caught trying to help them escape.

Hoping that they would not be caught, they would often sneak from one station to another. The stations would be separated by approximately 10 or 20 miles. They would often wait at a station until they knew the next one would be safe and could handle them.

❧

There is no documentation as to exactly how many escaped since they had to be very secretive. Some records indicate that over 100,000 of them escaped using the railroad, which includes the 30,000 escaping during the time prior to the Civil War.

CIVIL WAR

....

When Abraham Lincoln became president, the states towards the south became afraid that slavery would be outlawed. These states then seceded and formed the Confederacy.

This set off what became known as the Civil War. With the North winning the war, the southern states again became part of the Union. The Confederacy was formed by the southern states once they decided to secede.

Jefferson Davis became their president and they had a separate constitution. The Confederacy consisted of the states of South Carolina, Florida, Mississippi, Georgia, Alabama, Texas, Arkansas, Virginia, Tennessee, Louisiana, and North Carolina.

The North was comprised of the northern 25 states. They were also called the Union to represent that they desired the United States remain a single union. They were larger and had more industry. There was more resources, wealth, and people providing them advantage during the war.

The South worried that once the United States expanded, they would have less power. They wanted to have power and the ability to have their laws.

They feared they would lose the right to slaves. States in the north had already outlawed slavery and the south feared the U.S. would make it illegal in every state.

The deadliest war in our history was the Civil War. More than 600,000 soldiers perished in this war. It started in Fort Sumter, South Carolina on April 12, 1861. It ended April 9, 1865 as General Lee surrendered to Ulysses S Grant at the Appomattox Court House located in Virginia.

KEITH ROCCO

EMANCIPATION PROCLAMATION AND THE THIRTEENTH AMENDMENT

In 1863 President Lincoln signed the Emancipation Proclamation declaring that the slaves living in the Southern states were now free.

While this did not set all of them free immediately, it started the process. Since the Emancipation Proclamation was an Executive Order, it was not considered a part of the Constitution, but paved the way for the Thirteenth Amendment.

This Emancipation allowed Black men to fight for the Union Army. Approximately 200,000 black soldiers fought for the Union Army assisting in the North winning the war.

Lincoln thought that he would need a greater victory for support of the Emancipation. He felt that without support it would fail. He wanted a major victory in the North.

D uring the Battle of Antietam on September 17, 1862, when the Union Army reverted back, he knew the time had come. On September 22, 1862, an announcement was made that the order was about to become real.

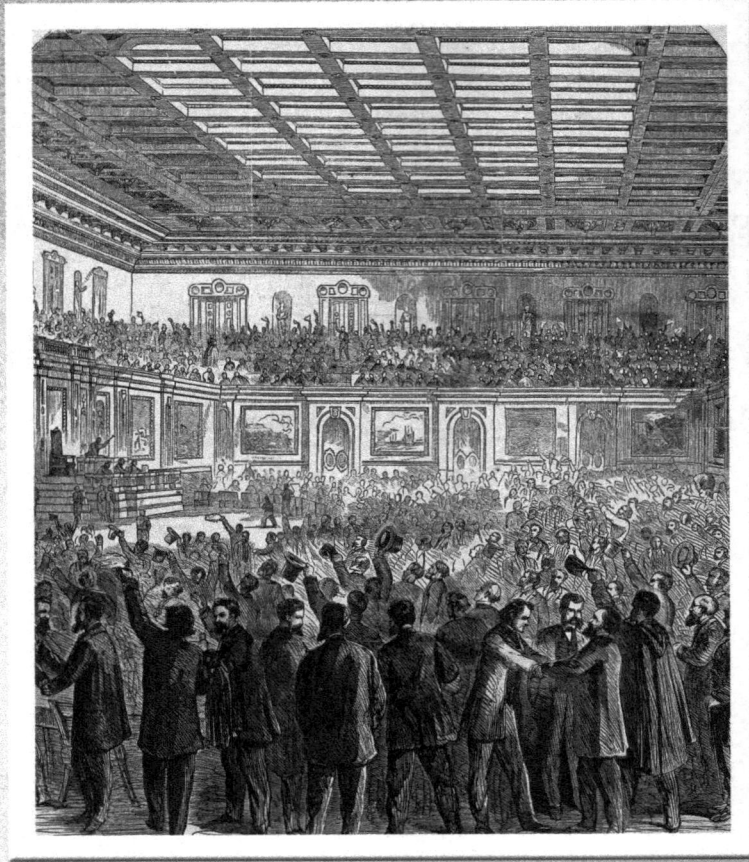

❧❦❧

On February 15, 1865, the Thirteenth Amendment was
sent for ratification. Georgia ratified the amendment
on December 6, 1865. With Georgia becoming the
27th state to ratify this amendment, it became enough
(three-fourths) to make it a portion of the Constitution.

Mississippi did not ratify it until 1995. It still allows that slavery is permitted as punishment of a crime. It also allows for a person to be prosecuted when forcing another person to work against their will.

ABOLITIONISM

....

Towards the end of the 1700s, The fight began to prohibit it in the United States. The people that wanted to stop it were named abolitionists since they desired abolishment of it.

In 1776, Rhode Island became the first state for abolishment, Vermont then followed during 1777, Pennsylvania then followed in 1780, and other northern states after.

The northern states became against it by 1820, but the southern states fought to keep it. The southern states became quite reliant on them. They were a large percentage of the population of the south (more than 50% in certain states).

In 1820, the Missouri Compromise was passed by Congress, allowing Missouri to be considered as a slave-state, but then Maine was admitted at the same time as a free state. Several northern states banned it after the American Revolution. Most of them living north were let free by 1840. Northern people thought it should not be allowed at all in the U.S. They were named abolitionists since they sought abolishment of slavery.

SLAVE STATES AND FREE STATES

The United States became separated between the slave states to the south and the free states in the north. As additional states became added, issues would arise as to whether it would be legalized. Several people became upset once Missouri became a state since it was a slave state. Congress then admitted Maine as a free state to even it out.

ABRAHAM LINCOLN

Lincoln served with the Illinois State Legislature for many terms. During this period, he studied law and started work as a lawyer. He then ran for the Congress in 1845. He won and served as congressman for one term. He then continued work as a lawyer. He then ran for the Senate, and while he lost, he did receive recognition for his fight against slavery during the debates.

Abraham Lincoln became President in 1860. The southern states feared he would favor abolishment of it. They then formed the Confederacy and this is when the Civil War began. He is most known for being in charge of the country throughout the American Civil War.

His leadership for the North helped the U.S. to be strong and be victorious over the South maintaining a united country. He then pushed to free all slaves throughout our nation. Probably best known for the Gettysburg Address, Lincoln gave this short speech on November 1, 1863.

President Lincoln died April 15, 1865, after he was shot by John Wilkes Booth while enjoying a play at the Ford Theatre in Washington D.C. There is still so much to learn about slavery and this era.

You can find more information by researching on the internet, and reaching out to your teachers, parents and friends.

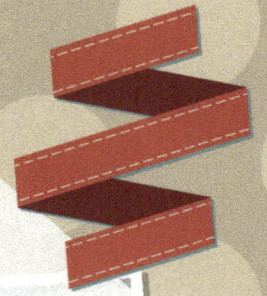

Visit

BABY PROFESSOR
EDUCATION KIDS

www.BabyProfessorBooks.com

to download Free Baby Professor eBooks
and view our catalog of new and exciting
Children's Books

Milton Keynes UK
Ingram Content Group UK Ltd.
UKHW050926310824
447642UK00002B/135

9 798869 402592